Pruning Trees, Shrubs & Vines

CONTENTS

Introduction

Do you have an old grapevine that needs training? A forsythia that has become too leggy? Have you just purchased a new home and felt mystified by the pruning chores ahead?

The subject of pruning can fill a whole book, and sometimes even the experts disagree over the best practices. But the principles of pruning are simple. This bulletin tells you how to keep your trees, shrubs, and vines attractive and healthy through careful pruning.

What is pruning? It is cutting away unwanted parts of a plant for a better shape or more fruitful growth.

What is involved in pruning? To do the job well, you need to know when (in what season) to prune, what to cut away, and how to do the cutting. For most jobs, all you will need are a few simple hand tools, although power tools are sometimes handy.

Is pruning really necessary? Nature does its own pruning. The woods are full of dead limbs and branches pruned by nature's ruthless wind, snow, and ice storms. Weak branches die and drop off neglected trees; rubbing branches kill one another. Thick undergrowth frequently kills trees by its dense shade. But, nature's pruning is a slow, haphazard process; you can get better results with pruning shears.

There are four basic reasons for pruning. Careful pruning enables you to control the shape and growth of your plant, to increase its productivity through more blooms and larger fruits, and to maintain the health of the plant.

Pruning for Shape and Form. Some pruning is done mainly for appearance. The beauty of conifers, such as fir, spruce, and pine trees lies in their natural shape. But these stiff-needled plants are actually forest trees, and frequently they will ruin the appearance of property by smothering the house, crowding doorways, or blocking off windows. Trees should be controlled by pruning.

With formal foundation plantings, the shrubs or trees are sheared, rather than pruned. Shearing means cutting off the soft new growth to limit the plant's growth and to shape it.

Heading back is a term you'll hear with respect to pruning for shape. It simply means reducing the size of a plant to encourage denser growth.

Growth Control. A young plant should be pruned to give it a basic structure of good habits and tendencies. In the case of a fruit tree, for example, you want to open up the tree to allow more

New trees or shrubs may come in a container, balled and burlapped, or bare-rooted. If bare-rooted, prune back the top (right) to restore balance.

sunlight to get to the inner branches so fruit can grow and ripen there, as well as on the outer limbs. A tree must be pruned to be strong enough to hold up its fruit load. You also prune to avoid a weak structure, as when a fruit tree develops a crotch that could split.

Pruning is necessary when a young tree is transplanted. A growing plant should be able to take up enough moisture through its roots to sustain itself. In transplanting, however, the digging out process frequently disturbs and destroys part of the root growth. Wilting will occur if the moisture given off by the foliage on the top of the plant exceeds the capacity of the roots to supply it. So pruning is done to keep the top growth down to what the roots can support.

Increase Productivity. A tree or bush has just so much energy to expend in producing blooms and fruits. If you thin out extra branches, you will have larger, showier blossoms and bigger fruits. A well-thinned fruit tree is more likely to bear every year, too.

Healthier Plants. It's a drain on the energy of any plant to support dead limbs and broken or diseased branches. These should come off promptly. A dead branch offers an opportunity for insects and rot organisms to enter.

When should you prune? When to prune depends on many things. First, it depends on the plant. Trees are usually pruned while they are dormant. If pruned in the spring — or even late winter — certain trees will bleed too much sap; others, if pruned in the summer or early fall, may develop new soft growth that will not withstand the winter. For these same reasons, grapevines are also pruned while dormant. Hedges, on the other hand, are trimmed several times a growing season to stimulate denser growth.

There are no absolute rules to follow. Many growers prefer to prune "heavy bleeders" — maples and birches — late in the summer. In areas where the winter is not severe, fall pruning may not lead to growth that can be winter-killed as it would in northern areas.

The growth habit of the plant is an important consideration. With flowering shrubs, you need to know whether blooms are produced on year-old growth or on new growth. Early spring pruning stimulates growth for shrubs that will bloom on the new shoots; but pruning after flowering is best for shrubs like forsythia that bloom on year-old wood.

Any time is a good time to prune away dead growth or broken or diseased limbs. Feel free to snip away water sprouts or remove suckers as they appear. Undesired growth drains energy from the plant.

The Basics

The mistake that many home growers make is usually either too little or too much pruning. The extent to which a plant needs to be pruned depends on the habits of the species and also on how old the plant is. A young tree, vine, or shrub will need more formative pruning to get it off to a good shape. Many ornamental trees and vines can be left pretty much alone once they have matured.

Check the table in the back of this bulletin for the special pruning requirements of many commonly grown plants. Always keep in mind to what purpose you are training your plant — as a privacy hedge or fruit-bearing tree, for example — and let your common sense guide you.

Tools

There is a large assortment of pruning equipment on the market, and only trial and error will enable you to find the tools you like to work with best. But a few hand tools will get you started.

Whether or not you want to invest in power tools is another decision. For most jobs, hand tools — shears, clippers, saws, and knives — will do. Pole pruners can extend your reach far enough for most jobs.

Pruning Equipment. *Pruning shears,* hand clippers, or hand pruners, as they are variously called, will be your most used and useful tools. Many gardeners make it a practice to carry a pair with them always. That way they are ready to snip off any unwanted water sprouts, suckers, or faded blooms.

The ideal pruning shear is lightweight, cuts easily, and makes clean cuts which heal over quickly. Some gardeners have several pairs; one kept especially sharp for fine pruning of roses and shrubs, and others for rough work like cutting roots and separating clumps of perennials.

Pruning shears come in a variety of styles. Some operate with a thin, sharp blade that cuts against an anvil. There is also a scissors-type pruner. Personal preference will determine which one is best for you.

Long-handled lopping shears will give you additional leverage and reach for taller, bigger branches. Some lopping shears are gear-driven for additional leverage. A *tree pruner,* for cutting those very high branches, up to an inch in diameter, is extremely useful on tall shrubs, and high-growing vines. These are simply clippers mounted on top of poles. The cutting action is activated by a rope and spring.

For large tree limbs, a *pruning saw* is necessary — an ordinary hand saw won't do, it tends to gum up. Pruning saws also come in a variety of styles. There are both straight-bladed and curved saws for general purpose work, and fine-tooth saws for finer work. A lightweight *bow saw* is also handy. A *pole saw* is similar to a pole pruner — it is a saw mounted on a long pole.

A sharp *knife* is another essential. It will enable you to trim wounds left when tree branches are removed.

Don't be tempted to use a heavy-duty pruner where a saw is appropriate. It may squeeze the branch rather than cut it, and the wound will be much greater. A good rule of thumb is a branch beyond one inch in diameter should be cut with a saw.

Shearing Equipment. Because shearing involves cutting soft growth, instead of wood, different tools are used. A *long-handled hedge shear,* electric- or hand-powered, is the main tool.

Make sure the model you choose is the right tone for the job you have to do. Are the handles long enough to enable you to reach the top of your shrub? Are the blades heavy enough to cut coarse-twigged shrubs, or will they just chew them up? Electric tools are handy for big jobs, and some electric hedge clippers are available without cords.

Maintenance. Keep your tools in good condition. Most blades can be kept sharp with a grindstone or whetstone. Saws should be sharpened professionally. Clippers and pruners need an occasional drop of motor oil to keep them operating smoothly. Protect the metal surfaces from rust by keeping them dry and occasionally oiled. Clean off sap and pitch with a little kerosene.

Pruning Terms

Axil: The angle formed by branch and leaf and the part of the plant from which it arises.

Bearing tree: A fruit tree that has reached the age of producing blossoms and fruits.

Branch: A shoot that has grown for more than one season.

Bud: An unexpanded flower or vegetative shoot. Buds may develop into flowers or into leaves and shoots. They may be terminal, as at the top of a shoot, or lateral, as in the axil of a leaf.

Candle: New terminal growth on a pine from which needles will emerge.

Cane: A long, healthy branch, usually referring to the growth on brambles or vines.

Central leader: A style of pruning that leaves one single, strong trunk from which side branches are allowed to grow.

Columnar: A tree that naturally grows in a tall, narrow shape.

Crotch: The angle between two branches or shoots near the point of their union.

Deshoot: Removal of young shoots from a tree during growing season to aid in training it to a desirable shape.

Disbud: Selective removal of flower buds so that the remaining buds become bigger and produce showier blooms.

Dormant: Resting, or not growing.

Espalier: A tree or shrub trained to grow flat against a trellis or wall.

Fruiting wood: Shoots or branches carrying flower buds and having the potential for bearing fruit.

Hanger: A drooping branch on a tree that does not normally have branches which grow downward. These should be removed.

Head: The extension of the tree trunk above the first branches.

Heading back: Cutting away a portion of the terminal growth of a branch or shoot, usually to control the size of the tree or shrub.

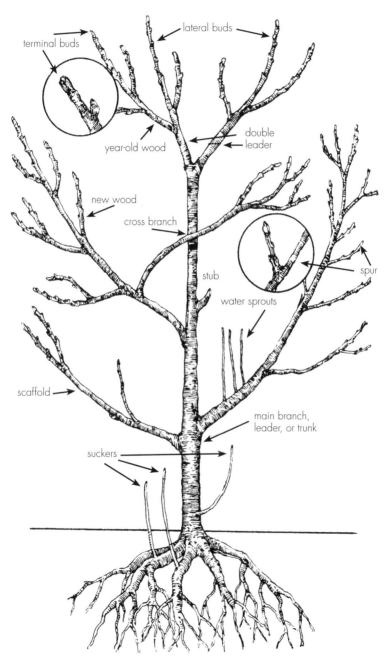

Anatomy of a tree.

Latent bud: A bud that does not break within the season it is formed. These may develop into new growth if existing branches are broken or pruned.

Lateral: A shoot or branch arising from a side (lateral) bud of another shoot or branch.

Lateral bud: A bud on the side rather than tip of a stem.

Leader: A developing trunk that is stronger and taller than any laterals.

Modified leader: A system of pruning, usually a fruit tree, where the central stem is kept part way up the tree, and then is allowed to branch more freely.

Open vase: A system of pruning, usually fruit trees, when the main trunk is kept short and the center of the tree is kept open, with the limbs growing around the open center.

Pinch: Heading a growing shoot by removing the top with your fingernails.

Pyramidal: A tree with a broad base tapering to a pointed top.

Scaffold: A branch arising from the trunk.

Scion: The cutting of one plant that is grafted to the rootstock of another.

Shoot: Vegetative growth produced from a bud, generally during the current growth season.

Spur: Short, thick growth producing flowers on apple, pear, and cherry trees.

Standard: A plant not normally grown as a tree that has been trained to a single trunk with a round head. Roses are often grown to a standard.

Stone fruit: Represented by peach, plum, apricot, and cherry.

Sucker: A vigorous shoot arising from the rootstock or from the lower portion of the trunk. These should be removed immediately.

Terminal bud: The bud at the end of the trunk or branch that extends the growth of the plant.

Topiary: To shape a tree or shrub into an unnatural form for ornamental purposes.

Water sprout: A vigorous shoot arising from a latent bud on the trunk or on older branches. These may be caused by overpruning and should be promptly removed.

How to Cut

The cardinal rule of pruning is *cut cleanly and leave no stubs.* A dead stub will rot, die, and is vulnerable to infections that can spread to the rest of the tree. Either cut close to the main branch or immediately above a bud.

Only the stub on the far left has been cut properly. From left to right: the first cut is done correctly; the second cut leaves too much surface; the third cut leaves too long a stub; and the fourth cut was made too close to the bud.

Make your pruning cut just above the bud that grows in the direction you want the new growth to take.

When cutting above a bud, which will stimulate new growth, make the cut just above a bud that grows in the direction the new growth is desired. A bud on the outside of a branch will grow out; one on the inside of a branch will grow in toward the center of the tree — usually an undesirable direction. The cut should be made close to the bud so it does not leave a long stub, and it should be angled, but not so sharply that it leaves a long, exposed surface.

When sawing off a sizeable limb, the main danger is that the limb will split off before you have completed your neat and clean saw cut. There is a simple three-step cutting method that avoids this hazard. Make a cut about one-third of the way through the branch, ten to fifteen inches out from the main trunk. Saw from the bottom up. A second cut is made farther out on the branch, this time from the top down and cutting all the way through. The limb will often break off, but the jagged edge will extend no farther than the first cut you made. Then cut the remaining stub flush and parallel to the main trunk.

After performing the cutting operation, any loose bark should be trimmed back to the point where it is sound and firmly adhered to the wood. For the quickest healing results, the wound should be trimmed clean with no ragged edges. Use your knife to smooth over the wound and surrounding bark.

Every cut of more than 1½ inches in diameter should have a protective coating of wound dressing. The primary reason for coating a large wound is to keep out moisture and to accelerate the healing process. Healing is quicker if the wound is trimmed in an oval shape. It sometimes takes years before a wound is covered with bark, so a seasonal repainting is advisable. Although any paint will seal out the insects and the effects of weather, a commercial tree-paint preparation contains antiseptic as an additional protection against disease.

Practical Pruning Tips

- Cut off a diseased, dead, or broken branch from any tree or plant at any time.
- Prune the weaker of two rubbing or interfering branches that are developing bark wounds — the quicker the better.
- Always prune flush to the parent branch or trunk. If only the end of a branch is dead, cut just beyond and close to a bud. Note: Be sure the branch is dead — not dormant — by slicing the bark and looking for green wood.
- In pruning, don't leave stubs or ragged cuts. Always use sharp, clean-cutting pruning tools.

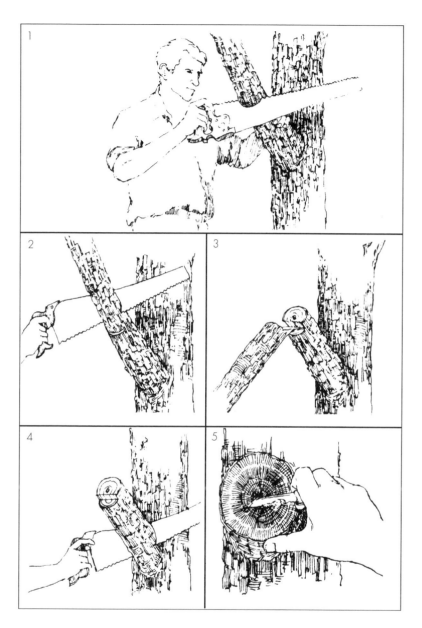

Step 1. Make a cut about one-third of the way through the branch, ten to fifteen inches out from the trunk. Step 2. Saw completely through the branch a few inches farther out on the branch. Step 3. The bark will tear only as far as the first cut. Step 4. Saw the remaining stub close to the trunk. Step 5. Trim the edges of the wound with a sharp knife.

- All bark-wounds over 1½ inches in diameter should have a protective coating of dark paint.
- Prune a hedge so that the plants grow wider at the base than at the top.
- Pruning top terminal branches produces a low spreading tree. By pruning lateral or side branches the tree will grow upwards — less bushy.
- Burn what you cut to avoid spreading disease and attracting rot organisms.
- Keep pruning shears sharp and well-oiled, and use the right tool for the job.
- In the garden it's always good practice to carry hand clippers.
- Keep trees out of foundation plantings. Never let trees and shrubs block windows of the house.
- Keep your feet on the ground. Don't use step ladders, chairs, or other make-shifts to prune the upper branches — use long-handled pruners or tree pruners and pole saws.
- Don't climb trees — it's too hazardous — that's the job for a professional arborist who has proper equipment and knows how to use it.

Special Care for Different Plants

Before you being pruning, consider what look you are aiming for. Are you pruning for the sake of appearance, to control growth, or to increase the productivity of the plant? Just as an artist will "rough out" a sketch before painting, many pruners will begin by roughing out the pruning shape they are trying to achieve.

Fruit Trees

First remove dead, broken, or diseased limbs. Next remove suckers, water sprouts, crossing limbs, and any other growth that appears to be crowding your plant or departing from the plant's desired shape. Work from the larger branches down to the finer cuts.

The experts disagree over the best time to prune a fruit tree; but most will concede that pruning while the tree is dormant is best. Whether that is in winter or early spring is your choice, but most orchardists do not like to prune on subzero days when the wood is frozen.

The young fruit tree starts life anew with a transplant, and in its first year it is cut back to a mere whip. After that initial cutting, very little pruning is done in its second and third year — until the plant begins to bear fruit.

What little pruning is done in this period is very necessary. Second and third year pruning determines the shape of the head, prevents the development of bad crotches, keeps a strong central trunk, and prevents the tree from getting too wide or too leggy. Be careful not to overprune at this stage — it will delay bearing and cause excessive wood growth.

The first year the height of the head should be established by cutting off the branches that grow lower down on the trunk than desired. Remember that a branch will become weighted down by fruit

Methods of Pruning

Just as each orchardist may disagree about the correct time to prune, each has his own method of pruning. If you turned a dozen loose, no two would trim your trees alike, yet each might do a good job.

Home fruit growers often get upset or discouraged at the complicated directions given in pruning books. Some of these give explicit rules for pruning to a leader, a modified leader, or an open vase shape. Don't let these terms throw you. In fact, I wouldn't even worry about them at all, because many veteran fruit growers have pruned for years and never heard of them.

If you want to get technical, pruning to a leader means simply keeping a strong central trunk in the middle of the tree and letting all the other branches come from it. A modified leader means that the central stem is kept partway up the tree, then allowed to branch more freely, growing several tops on the tree. An open vase means that the center of the tree is kept open and limbs are allowed to grow around this open space, letting plenty of sun into all of them.

Generally speaking, trees that produce large fruit — such as apples, pears, and peaches — do better when grown with a strong central or modified leader. Apricots, cherries, and plums, which are less likely to split from heavy fruit loads, are more suitable for the open vase treatment.

Lewis Hill, *Fruits and Berries for the Home Garden,* Storey Publishing.

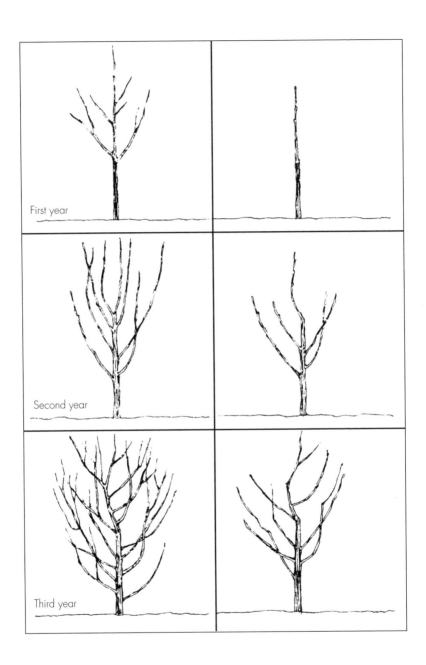

Training a young fruit tree to a strong central leader. In its first year, it is cut back to a strong leader; in its second year, primary scaffold branches are allowed to develop; in its third year, it has reached its mature form.

First year

Second year

Third year

or ice and snow. It is important to keep lowest branches from touching the ground. The remaining side limbs may be shortened but retained, if they are well distributed. Not more than two should be left that arise near any one point on the trunk, because of the danger of splitting later on. Except on peach and cherry trees, these side limbs should be cut back from one-third to one-half at planting time.

In the second and following years, attention should be directed toward the removal of vigorous growth that tends to crowd, compete with, or injure the main limbs of the tree.

After the fruit tree begins to bear fruit, more pruning will be desirable to keep the branches well balanced. The kind of pruning needed at this time will be, largely, cutting back the lateral branches in the top and thinning out. With peaches, the cutting back is often carried into one- or two-year old, or even older, wood.

Some trees produce their fruits along the branches, while others tend to do most of their bearing on short, stubby spurs. Many of the stone fruits belong to this spur-type of tree; and in recent years, some spur-type apple trees have been developed. The important thing to remember when pruning spur-type fruit trees is that some of the excess spurs should be removed, but be sure not to remove too many or your yield will be reduced.

Apple and Peach Trees. In shaping young orchard trees, the main stem is pruned back to make a low head. As the tree matures, the small branches, which have a tendency to grow towards the center of the tree, should be pruned back close to the parent limb to admit sunlight into the open head. These low, umbrella-shaped trees are more easily sprayed, the fruit ripens more readily and is easier to harvest.

Apple trees have a tendency to sprout soft young shoots from the side branches. These water sprouts should be pruned close to their base when they appear.

The yearling peach tree is generally cut to a whip about three feet high at planting time. If the side branches are very well developed, they may be cut back to two or three buds.

Other Fruits. An upright compact form is natural for the pear tree. Each spring a light thinning is advisable. The cut should be made above an outside bud so that new growth will have an outward tendency. Most pear trees can be handled like the apple, but less pruning is desirable because of the danger of blight.

For cherry trees, it seems best to thin out the scaffold limbs (branches growing from main trunk) where necessary, but not to cut them back unless the basal buds on the branches are in good condition.

The Japanese plums are handled much like the peach, while other plum and cherry trees need to be pruned more nearly like the apple.

Reviving a Neglected Fruit Tree. Bringing an old fruit tree into production after years of neglect requires much effort. But if you have recently bought an old farm, you may find yourself the proud owner of a lovely, old, overgrown orchard. Having weighed the pros and cons of the operation and decided to try and restore the orchard, you'll need to prune those trees worth saving.

Resist the temptation to prune heavily at first. The tree could easily be shocked by any drastic operation. The first pruning should remove broken limbs, rubbing or diseased branches, and all sucker growths from the base of the tree. Take all the usual precautions so that the large limbs don't strip bark from the tree as they fall. And be sure to coat the wounds with a tree dressing.

Only in the second year of reclaiming should any cutting of healthy wood be done. This light pruning should be done to improve the shape of the tree. Because you are removing parts of the tree that bears fruit, the tree will be able to put more energy in the remaining limbs, so you should gain in fruit size and quality.

By the third year and thereafter, you can prune in the normal, annual way.

Grapes

Few plants respond to pruning more than grapevines. An over-grown, dense, unpruned vine will not receive enough light to ripen grapes well. Also, because the fruit is borne mostly on year-old wood, it is necessary to maintain an annual supply.

Grapes are pruned while the vine is dormant; usually this means early spring or late winter. Never handle a frozen cane; it is brittle and will snap off. If your winters are severe, and you expect a certain percentage of canes killed by the cold, don't prune until the early spring when you can see which canes made it through the winter. If you handle the canes after spring growth has begun, however, you are almost certain to injure the tender buds.

Grapes will grow most anywhere in good, well-drained soil. The vines can be trained to any number of different systems involving

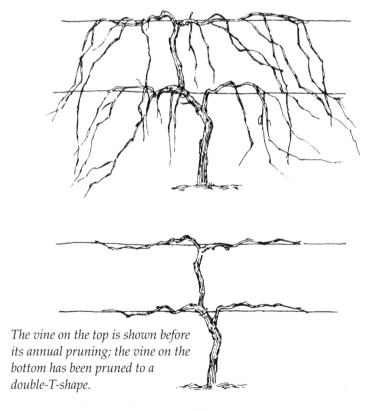

The vine on the top is shown before its annual pruning; the vine on the bottom has been pruned to a double-T-shape.

an arbor or trellis. In fact the different systems could fill a book; different varieties are best suited for different trellis styles. The Four-Cane Kniffen System is preferred by many growers and it is as well adapted to the home garden. The supports for this trellis consist of two horizontal wires — the lower one runs about thirty inches and the upper sixty inches from the ground. The wires should be well-braced to prevent sagging.

Under the Four-Cane Kniffen System, the vine is trained to have one sturdy trunk supporting a double-T-shaped arrangement of canes. Once the vine is established, annual pruning should be done in early spring to remove the canes that bore fruit the previous season. What is left is four new canes to bear fruit.

When the young grape plant is first set out it should be cut back to one vigorous cane of two or three buds — which will leave the plant about five or six inches tall. It is advisable to stake the cane to keep it upright and straight, as it is to become the main trunk that will support the four fruit-bearing canes.

The second and third year all side shoots that have developed on the main trunk should come off, except the two near the upper wire and the two near the lower wire. These should be cut back to three or four buds each and tied to the wires. They will form a double-T-shape. Pinch off any other buds as they appear.

Each season thereafter, the vine should be pruned back to four canes, and each cane should be cut to eight or ten buds, from which the season's new growth will be made.

Pruning of older established vines will be much the same procedure, except that two spurs of two buds each are left at the base of each cane for renewal the following year of the four original canes. Each year, the four best canes which developed form these spurs should be selected to replace the previous year's canes.

An old grapevine may be cut nearly to the ground and a new trunk started from one of the new shoots. This will, of course, mean the sacrifice of a year's crop — but it is worth it.

Treated well, each mature vine should last about fifty years, producing an annual harvest of twelve to fifteen pounds of grapes — or thirty to sixty bunches. Don't allow your vines to overproduce; you'll sacrifice quality. Instead pinch off extra bunches before they develop.

Berries

Strawberries. New plants are usually sold bare-rooted with instructions for pruning back the roots to encourage more vigorous growth. Trim the roots back so that they are three to four inches long. Also, remove any old leaves or blossom buds before planting.

During the plant's first season, pinch off any blossoms that develop to prevent the young plant from setting fruit. The blossom stems should be removed entirely, snipping or pinching them off at the base of the plant.

As soon as they are established, the new plants will send out runners. For extra-large quality berries, remove all runners before they root. For large yields, allow four or five runners from each plant to develop a "matted row" not more than two feet wide. Cut back any runners that have a tendency to run out of bounds in the paths.

Berries are harvested the second and third years. After that the bed runs out and should be plowed under and replaced by a new planting in a different location.

Bramble Berries. There is a bewildering assortment of raspberries — red, black, purple, and yellow — and blackberries that the homeowner can raise easily. Most bramble berries produce fruit only on year-old canes. These new canes grow vigorously during the summer, initiate flower buds in the fall, and then bear fruit the following season. The canes begin to die shortly after the fruit is harvested. The dead canes should be cut and burned. Since the roots live on, new shoots will grow each spring and summer and repeat the cycle, providing next year's fruiting canes.

Set your new raspberry plants deeper than they were in the nursery to cover the cane buds. One leader can remain above the ground and should be cut back to about eight to twelve inches. Leave the soil loose at the surface of the ground so that the buried canes can emerge. After the row is set with new plants — it should be kept to no more than eighteen inches wide — all traveling suckers growing outside the row should be removed with a hoe or cut out with a spade. The canes should be at least six inches apart in a row.

Pruning bramble berries takes place twice a year. The second year after planting, the spring pruning should consist of cutting back all plants to two inches above the ground. This encourages maximum cane growth for big crops the next year. In the fall, cut the tops of the

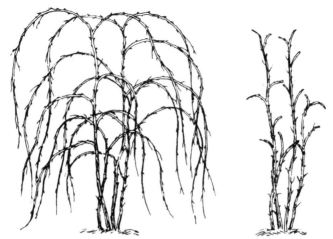

Black raspberry before pruning and after it is pruned back to four sturdy canes.

plants back so that the canes are about four to five feet tall.

After that, your twice-a-year pruning should take place in late summer and fall. In late summer, cut the canes that bore fruit and now look pallid and brittle to the ground level. Thin the new canes to six inches apart. Remove any short and weak canes. Just before winter, cut back the canes to four feet in height. You may want to put up wire to support your bushes.

Hand clippers are the best tool to use for pruning these berries. Gloves will protect your hands from thorns. Be sure to *burn* the cut canes. This will prevent the spread of disease and insects.

Bush Berries. The bush berries — blueberries, gooseberries, elderberries, chokecherries, high bush cranberries, and huckleberries — require very little pruning, but they should be thinned out every few years. All older branches as well as dead and weak ones should be removed, and the young fruiting shoots trimmed back if the bush is spreading too wide. Elderberries and chockcherries have a tendency to spread. Sometimes mowing down all the prolific suckers is the only way to keep your elderberry in line.

Shade Trees

In general, mature shade trees require very little pruning — except for removing dead branches and thinning out dense growth. But a young tree requires some attention to ensure that it grows in a desirable shape.

Shade tree is a broad term and covers trees that grow in a variety of natural forms: columnar, pyramidal, round, spreading, and weeping. Know which shape your mature tree will take.

As a rule of thumb, columnar trees, like poplars, and pyramidal trees, like firs, should be allowed to keep their lower branches. But spreading trees, like oaks, and round trees, Norway maples for example, look better with their bottom branches removed, unless they are being used as a screen. A weeping tree, such as a willow, should be pruned so that its lowest branches do not touch the ground.

Shade trees are pruned with the same general principles as fruit trees. It is necessary to thin out branches when they grow too densely, gradually removing lower branches. Limbs that form a bad crotch should be cut away so that the tree won't develop a double leader. The elm, however, is an exception to this rule as it forms a crotch naturally. Outside of emergency operations it is not wise to prune shade trees during the period when sap is flowing. Some trees such as birches, elms, and maples bleed heavily when pruned in late winter and spring. Late summer, after all new growth has stopped, is the proper time to prune trees of this type, as well as willows, oaks, ashes, and sycamores.

Evergreens

Unless grown as a hedge, or kept small for some other reason, conifers, such as fir, balsam, spruce, and pine trees, should not be severely pruned or sheared. Their natural pyramid form is their beauty. To thicken the growth of conifers, it is advisable to shear the center tips, or candles, of the top and side branches. This should be done during the early summer.

Small evergreens in foundation plantings can be controlled and kept well in hand by shearing the end buds and leaders. The softer-foliaged evergreens such as yews, arborvitae, junipers, and retinisporas are adapted to shearing to a smooth surface and various forms. Such formal shearing, however, is not considered good practice. Low growing forms of juniper and others, should they start to intrude on a path or lawn, can be sheared back to a lusty side shoot or the leaders can be pruned out. In any event, foundation plantings of trees or shrubs should never be allowed to grow high enough to cover the windows.

Broad-leaved evergreen shrubs such as rhododendron and laurel need little pruning except to preserve the natural shape of the plant and remove all dead or broken branches. Old, dilapidated, spindly plants can be cut to the ground to encourage new shoots. The clipping of old, faded flowers back to an axil bud is essential for continued bloom. Young plants should be clipped occasionally to encourage sturdy growth. Old, overgrown plants of some varieties can be cut back severely in early spring.

Should the leader, or topmost shoot, of an evergreen be injured by storm or have to be cut away, the tree will not cease its upward growth. Gradually, one of the stronger, radiating side branches that grows from the main stem at the base of the lost tip will grow faster than the others, straighten up little by little, and in time replace the lost leader. This natural replacement effort can be hastened by taking the most promising side shoot, gently bending it upward and tying it in that position to a splint bound to the main stem. Under this gentle pressure it will become upright more rapidly and dominate over the others, and the tree will regain its natural shape.

Ornamental Shrubs and Vines

Flowering shrubs are planted for their colorful bloom and usually require little pruning. They are most beautiful when allowed to take their natural, untrammeled shapes.

When winter injury necessitates removal of part of a shrub, or if long neglect calls for a major thinning out, it is best to prune the oldest and poorest branches right back to the ground and shorten the others to reasonable lengths to keep the plant from becoming leggy or straggly. It is not good practice to trim all the lower branches and the young shoots coming up around the base of the plant, nor to give the plant a "barber shop haircut" — rounding off of a shrub until it has the outline of a mushroom or igloo. This makes an unnatural, grotesque thing of it; reduces its flowering area; and creates an effect that can be corrected only by demolishing the top and starting all over again.

When to prune a shrub depends on whether it is a spring-flowering or summer-/fall-flowering shrub. Spring-flowering shrubs, like forsythia, produce blooms on wood grown the previous season. It should be pruned immediately after blooming to allow new growth of wood for next season's blooms.

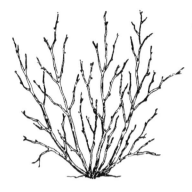

Shrub, before and after pruning.

Summer- and fall-flowering shrubs bloom on wood grown during the current season. Prune these shrubs either after blooming or wait until early spring. If you prune in early spring, you must find the time when frost is no longer a possibility, but spring growth hasn't begun either.

Lilacs should be pruned after flowering. Unless kept in control, they have a tendency to grow too tall and become leggy. Most of the young suckers and all the dead wood should come out. From time to time remove some of the older branches so that more light reaches the center. An old, uncared-for lilac should be cut nearly to the ground and restarted as an entirely new plant. A lilac that is allowed to become too dense is forced to grow high. Each branch should have growing room and the plant kept down to six to eight feet in height.

The stems that carry blooms should be pruned as soon as the flowers begin to fade. The cut should be made on the flowering twigs just above the first pair of axil buds. This also applies to rhododendron, buddleia, magnolia, and azalea.

Since the purpose of woody vines is usually to drape, clothe, or screen objects it is rarely desirable to prune them, except to induce new growth at the base or keep them under control. As always, dead wood should be cut out at any time and precocious shoots should be kept within bounds. Other than this, the less shears are used, the better.

Wisterias are often slow and reluctant to flower. Sometimes this is an inherent fault of the individual plant and cannot be overcome. Often, however, a rather severe heading back of the side shoots in midsummer or early autumn is effective. Root pruning with a sharp pointed spade around the main stem will also stimulate the formation of flowering buds that should provide a wealth of color the following spring.

Check the table for pruning times of various shrubs.

Pruning Time Table

Prune After Flowering

Akebia (chocolate vine)
Amelanchier (shadblow, serviceberry)
Calycanthus floridus (Carolina allspice)
Caragana (Siberian pea)
Celastrus (Bittersweet)
Cercis (American eastern redbud)
Chaenomoles (flowering quince)
Chionanthus (white fringe)
Cornus (dogwood)
Crataegus laevigata (English hawthorne)
Cydonia (quince)
Cytisus (broom)
Daphne
Deutzia
Exochorda (pearlbush)
Forsythia
Hamamelis (witch hazel)
Hydrangea (big-leaf hydrangea)
Kalmia (mountain laurel)
Kerria (Japanese kerria)
Kolwitzia amabilis (beautybush)
Lindera benzoin (spicebush)
Lonicera fragantissima (winter honey-suckle, fragrant honeysuckle)

Magnolia (cucumber tree)
Philadelphus (mock-orange)
Pieris (mountain andromeda)
Potentilla (shrubby cinquefoil)
Prunus (flowering almond, cherry, plum)
Rhododendron (azalea, rhododendron)
Ribes (flowering current)
Rosa (rose)
Spiraea, spring-flowering
Spiraea prunifolia (bridal wreath)
Spiraea thunbergii (Thunberg spiraea)
Spiraea x vanhouttei
Syringa (lilac)
Syringa reticulata (Japanese tree lilac)
Tamarix, spring-flowering
Viburnum carlesii (Korean spice viburnum)
Viburnum lantana (wayfaring tree)
Viburnum opulus (European cranberrybush)
Weigela (old-fashioned weigela)

Prune While Dormant

Abelia
Acanthopanax (fiveleaf aralia)
Althaea, shrubby (marsh mallow)
Amorpha (false indigo)
Baccharis (grounsel)
Berberis (barberry)
Buddleja davidii (butterfly bush)
Callicarpa (beautyberry)
Caryopteris (bluebeard)
Ceanothus (California lilac)

Clethra (summersweet)
Hibiscus (rose of Sharon)
Hydrangea (except H. macrophilia)
Hypericum (St. Johnswort)
Indigofera (indigo)
Lagerstroemia (crape myrtle)
Lespedeza (bush clover)
Ligustrum (privet)
Lonicera (berried honeysuckles)
Lycium (matrimony vine)

Rhus (sumac)
Rosa (hybrid tea roses)
Salix (willow)
Spiraea, summer-flowering
Spiraea japonica ('Anthony Waterer')
Spiraea douglasii (hardback pink
  spiraea)

Staphylea (bladdernut)
Stephanandra
Tamarix, late-flowering
Viburnum, berry-bearing
Vitex (chaste tree)

Hedges

Hedges are of two general classifications. Shrubs or trees planted close together in a row to form an informal hedge, wind-break, or high screen should be allowed to retain their original form and characteristics. Pruning of this type of hedge is confined to heading back for density and the removal of broken, diseased, or dead branches. The formal or "wall of green" type of hedge, such as Privet, Boxwood, and Japanese Barberry, takes kindly to close persistent pruning and shearing.

Newly Planted Hedges. Proper fashioning from the very beginning will result in a uniform foliage density from top to bottom. In planting a hedge the plants are usually set out close together in two staggered rows. It is a mistake to allow the plants to reach their desired height before pruning. This is usually the reason for so many poor, unsightly hedges with thin, sparse branching at the bottom.

As soon as the plants are set they should be cut back one-third of their height. When about twenty-four to thirty inches high, they should be cut back again six to twelve inches or nearly in half. This pruning encourages new growth from side buds and induces much desired branchlets and twigs in abundance. When this new growth is about a foot long it should be cut back again, about in half.

Each pruning makes the hedge grow thicker and broader. By the second or third season the new growth is usually large and dense enough to have permanent outline and dimensions. Two or three seasonal shearings are usually sufficient — the first as soon as growth starts in the spring, and the second and third in early and late summer. Pruning a hedge later than that is apt to stimulate new tender growth that is susceptible to winterkill. The base of the hedge should always be pruned wider than the top so that the lower branches get plenty of light, retain their foliage, and do not get straggly.

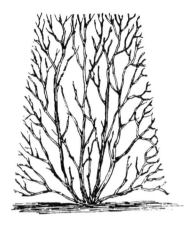 

The hedge bush on the left has been correctly pruned. A hedge bush should always be wider at the base than at the top.

Roses

Roses are pruned to increase new growth, renew vigor, or to control old growth and general appearance. But authorities do not agree on any one general rule for rose pruning, except that all roses should be kept young by cutting back old non-productive canes.

Various varieties call for different pruning treatments. Some types are cut back little or none — except for dead, broken, or surplus branches — while others do better pruned more or less severely, depending upon what the gardener wishes to accomplish.

Most roses bloom more luxuriantly on wood that is not more than two years old. The roots may be old, but the foliage above ground should usually be kept young.

Certain roses bloom on new wood; others flower on older canes. When an old cane has accomplished its usefulness in life and no longer bears roses, it should come out at the base in a clean slanting cut. Any excessively long canes should also be cut back in the fall to prevent winter damage. Severe pruning in the autumn, however, is not good practice; but nearly all roses are improved by thinning out in the spring. Roses of weak, straggly growth should be cut back more severely than the more vigorous growers.

Your rose bush should be cut back severely when you plant it, unless you bought it in a pot. Cut it back to about six to eight inches.

Be sure you cut to a bud and leave no dead stumps.

Teas and Hybrid Teas bloom on wood of the current year. Consequently, all old wood should be removed each spring back to five or six inches above the winter soil mound. Light fall pruning, when the canes may be shortened to about thirty inches, is advisable to prevent wind whipping and storm damage.

Hybrid Perpetual is a more rugged, vigorous plant than the Hybrid Tea. Each year it also blooms on shoots arising from stems of the previous year. When used as a bedding plant, however, perpetuals can be cut back to ten to fifteen inches in the spring, or even shorter. When used as a shrub, cut to two to three feet as desired. Pillar roses can be allowed to grow to any height, but cut out surplus wood to keep plant within bounds. A weak plant always requires harder pruning than a strong specimen.

Floribundas and Polyanthas are bush roses that produce clusters of bloom from early summer to late frost. The bedding roses of the Floribunda class grow to an average height of two to three feet. They should be pruned lightly, thinning out all dead and surplus wood in the late fall. Faded cluster heads should also be removed.

Rugosa Roses and their hybrids grow to a height of four to five feet, and the shrub types should have old canes cut out and new canes shortened to about two to four feet. Shrub roses other than Rugosa require little pruning. Elongated branches that have become out of hand can be pruned back to size in late fall or early spring. Many Old Fashioned Roses bear flowers on old wood. The pruning operation consists of a thinning out of old wood in the spring and leaving the huskiest one-year- and two-year-old canes. For finer bloom the plants can be pruned back to two and a half to three feet.

Ramblers or small-flowered climbers bloom on year-old wood; consequently, all the canes that have flowered should be removed as soon as the flowers fade. The current year's young canes produced from the base should be trained up to bloom the following season.

Climbing Roses of the large-flowered type bloom on older canes; so contrary to the Rambler variety, it is not advisable to remove all the canes that have flowered. Side shoots which have flowered can be cut back and all worn-out canes removed.

Cutting Roses. A single rose should be cut with an eye to stimulating future flowering and to preserve the shape of the plant. Each bud located in the axils of the leaves on the stems will send out a shoot that will bear another rose. The stem should be cut just above the second leaf joint, leaving only two groups of leaves below the

Leave no more than two groups of leaves below the cut on the branch. The figure on the left shows the first cutting; the figure on the right, the second cutting.

cut on each branch from which new growth will start. Cutting on shorter stems leaving several buds makes for too much competition of the shoots, and results in smaller, secondary blooms. Carefully located pruning stimulates flower production.

Condensed Pruning Guide

Fruits

	When	**How**
Apple	Winter or early spring	Train tree for low head. Prune moderately. Keep tree open with main branches well spaced around tree. Avoid sharp V-shaped crotches.
Blackberry	After bearing and summer	Remove at ground canes that bore last crop. In summer cut back new shoots 3½ feet high.

Raspberry	After bearing and in summer	Remove at the ground in fall canes which bore last crop. In summer head back new canes 20 inches to 22 inches high.
Cherry	Winter or early spring	Prune moderately, cut back slightly the most vigorous shoots.
Currant	Early spring	Remove old unfruitful growth. Encourage new shoots.
Gooseberry	Early spring	Same as currant. Cut back new shoots at 12 inches high and side shoots to two buds.
Grape	Late winter or early spring, before sap starts	Requires heavy pruning of old wood to encourage new bearing wood. Remove all old branches back to main vine. Cut back the previous year's new growth to four buds.
Peach	Early spring	Prune vigorously — remove one-half of the previous year's growth, keep tree headed low, and well thinned-out.
Plum	Early spring	Remove dead and diseased branches, keep tree shaped up by cutting back rank growth. Prune moderately.
Quince	Early spring	Cut back young trees to form low, open head. Little pruning of older trees required except to remove dead and weak growth.

	When	How
Barberry	Early spring	Little pruning required except to remove a few old branches occasionally to encourage new growth. Head back as necessary to keep plant in shape.
Butterfly Bush	Early spring	Cut out all dead wood. Remove some old branches and head-in as necessary to keep plant properly shaped.
Clematis	Spring	Cut out weak growth but save as much old wood as possible.
Crab	Early spring	Prune moderately. Cut out dead and broken branches and suckers.
Deutzias	After flowering	Remove a few older branches and all dead wood. Do not let growth get too dense.
Dogwood, Flowering	After flowering	Remove dead wood only.
Dogwood, Other	Spring	Varieties grown for colored twigs should have the old growth removed to encourage bright colored new shoots.
Elderberry	After fruiting	Prune severely. Remove one-half of season's growth.

Forsythia	After flowering	Remove a few older branches at the ground each year and head back new growth as necessary.
Honeysuckle, Bush	After fruiting	Cut out some old branches. Keep bush open.
Hydrangea	Early spring	Hills of Snow variety: cut back to ground. Others: remove dead and weak growth, cut old flowering stems back to two buds.
Laurel, Mountain	After flowering	Prune very little. Remove a few old branches at the ground from weak, leggy plants to induce growth from the roots.
Lilac	After flowering	Remove diseased and scaly growth, cut off old flower heads, and cut out surplus sucker growth.
Mock-Orange	After flowering	Cut out dead wood and a few old branches to thin out plant.
Rhododendron	After flowering	Treat same as Laurel, Mountain.
Roses, Climbing	After flowering	Cut out about one-half of old growth at the ground and retain the vigorous new shoots from the root for next year's flowers. Head back as necessary.

Roses: Tea, Hybrid, Perpetual	Spring after frosts	Cut away all dead and weak growth and shorten all remaining branches or canes to four buds for weak growers and five buds for vigorous varieties.
Rose of Sharon	When buds start	Cut out all winter killed growth back to live wood.
Snowberry	Early spring	Thin out some old branches and cut back last season's growth of that part remaining to three buds.
Trumpet Vine	Early spring	Prune side branches severely to the main stem.
Weigela	After flowering	Prune lightly, remove all dead, weak growth and head in as necessary. Cut out a few old branches at the ground to induce new growth.
Wisteria	Spring	Cut back the new growth to the spurs at the axils of the leaves. This can be repeated in midsummer.
Viburnum	Early spring	Prune lightly. Remove all dead, weak and a few of the old branches.
Virginia Creeper	Spring	Clip young plants freely. Older plants require little pruning except to remove dead growth and some thinning.